THE GIFT
BOOK

THE GIFT BOOK

MICHAEL O'MARA BOOKS LIMITED

First published in Great Britain
in 2009 by
Michael O'Mara Books Limited
9 Lion Yard
Tremadoc Road
London SW4 7NQ

A CIP catalogue record for this book
is available from the British Library.

ISBN 978-1-84317-407-3

1 2 3 4 5 6 7 8 9 10

www.mombooks.com

Printed and bound in China
by WKT

'A hug is the perfect gift;
one size fits all and nobody
minds if you exchange it.'

ANONYMOUS

ON FRIENDSHIP

And a youth said, Speak to us of Friendship.
And he answered, saying:
Your friend is your needs answered.
He is your field, which you sow with love and reap with thanksgiving.
And he is your board and your fireside.
For you come to him with your hunger, and you seek him for peace.

When your friend speaks his mind you fear not the 'nay' in your own mind, nor do you withhold the 'ay'.

And when he is silent your heart
ceases not to listen to his heart;
For without words, in friendship,
all thoughts, all desires, all
expectations are born and
shared, with joy that is
unclaimed.

FROM *THE PROPHET*
BY KHALIL GIBRAN

JOSEPH ADDISON

Author and politician Joseph
Addison once leant a good friend
some money to tide him over in
hard times. A few weeks later
Addison noticed that, whereas
in the past when he and his
friend discussed worldly matters

they always used to disagree on various subjects, now his friend was agreeing with everything he said. One day, Addison decided to choose a subject on which he knew that his friend held a completely opposing view from him, saying, 'Either contradict me, sir, or pay me my money!'

'The value of a man resides in what he gives and not in what he is capable of receiving.'
ALBERT EINSTEIN

HOW EXTREMELY EXTRAVAGANT!

Some gifts are better than others, and this certainly applies to the following story. In the 1870s, an eccentric American newspaper owner called James Gordon Bennett launched an edition of the *New York Herald* (which went on to become the *International Herald Tribune*) in Paris. One day, while travelling on the Train Bleu through France, Bennett tipped the train guard $14,000. According to legend at the next station the guard promptly stepped off the train, handed in his notice and bought himself a restaurant!

FRIENDS IN HIGH AND LOW PLACES

Singer-songwriter Tom Petty told the following story about his friend the country and western singer Johnny Cash: 'One of my favourite stories is being at this studio in downtown Hollywood – which is kind of a weird neighbourhood – when John came in with June … He was laughing, so I said, "Hey, where you been?"

He said, "June and I thought it would be fun to just sit on that bus bench across the street for a while. I met the most interesting people over there."

I said, "You're kidding me!" I was trying to picture the look on

these people's faces as they came
to wait for the bus, and there's
Johnny and June. This guy was
friends with presidents and he
was friends with people at the
bus stop.'

'I count myself in nothing
else so happy
As in a soul remembering
my good friends.'
FROM *RICHARD II*, WILLIAM
SHAKESPEARE

NOW, THAT'S SMART!

One Christmas mum decided she wasn't going to remind the kids about their thank you letters ... so grandma didn't receive the note to thank her for the generous cheque she'd sent.

The following year, things were different. 'This year the children came round to thank me in person,' gran told her friend.

'That's marvellous! What do you think caused the change in behaviour?'

'Oh, that's easy,' said gran. 'This year I didn't sign the cheques!'

AN IRISH BLESSING

May there always be work for your hands to do, may your purse always hold a coin or two. May the sun always shine on your windowpane, may a rainbow be certain to follow each rain. May the hand of a friend always be near you, may God fill your heart with gladness to cheer you.

'We should give as we would receive, cheerfully, quickly, and without hesitation; for there is no grace in a benefit that sticks to the fingers.'

SENECA

BE A FRIEND

'Be a friend. You don't need money:
Just a disposition sunny;
Just the wish to help another
Get along some way or other;
Just a kindly hand extended
Out to one who's unbefriended;
Just the will to give or lend,
This will make you
someone's friend.'

EDGAR A. GUEST

SCENARIOS
TO AVOID

He thinks: I'll buy her some of that
expensive anti-wrinkle cream
she likes.
She thinks: He thinks I'm looking
old.

She thinks: I know he needs socks.
He thinks: She's turning into my
mother.

He thinks: What about those lovely
slippers?
She thinks: He doesn't fancy me
any more.

She thinks: That aftershave is so
lovely.

He thinks: Do I smell so bad?

He thinks: Garden vouchers – she loves to potter around outside.

She thinks: Has he no imagination whatsoever?

She thinks: That beautiful paperweight would keep his papers tidy.

He thinks: She's turning into my sister.

> 'Think where man's glory most begins and ends, And say my glory was I had such friends.'
> W. B. YEATS

FRIENDS IN ADVERSITY?

Nineteenth-century art critic, John Ruskin, was always at pains to point out that even if he gave a terrible review about an artist's work, it shouldn't affect his friendship with that artist. However, the artists themselves weren't quite so eager to agree with Ruskin. 'Next time I meet you I shall knock you down,' one such friend reportedly said, 'but I trust it will make no difference to our friendship.'

'The best way to keep
your friends is not to
give them away.'
WILSON MIZNER

SAYING THANK YOU

Despite email and texting and
all the other fast methods of
communication, you will find that
there's nothing quite like a thank-
you note to keep your nearest
and dearest onside! It's not just an
old-fashioned thing, saying thank
you in a handwritten note is a sign
of good manners and respect, and
taking the time to write (and, let's

face it, it doesn't actually take *that* long) and post a letter will perk up the recipient's day.

❧

'It is great to have friends when one is young, but indeed it is still more so when you are getting old. When we are young, friends are, like everything else, a matter of course. In the old days we know what it means to have them.'

EDVARD GRIEG

❧

AULD LANG SYNE

*Should auld acquaintance
   be forgot,
And never brought to mind?
Should auld acquaintance
   be forgot,
And auld lang syne?*

*For auld lang syne, my dear,
For auld lang syne,
We'll tak a cup o' kindness yet,
For auld lang syne.*

ROBERT BURNS

SHAW VERSUS SIR WINSTON

Being able to tease one's friends and enjoy playful badinage is all part and parcel of friendship, as the following anecdote illustrates.

Eminent playwright George Bernard Shaw once sent his friend, Winston Churchill, a couple of tickets for the first night of his play, *St Joan*, together with a little note saying, 'One for yourself, the other for a friend – if you have one.'

Regrettably, Churchill couldn't make it on the night, so he sent Shaw a note explaining that he was otherwise engaged but that he would like tickets for the second night – 'If there is one'.

*'But friendship is precious,
not only in the shade, but in the
sunshine of life, and thanks to a
benevolent arrangement the greater
part of life is sunshine.'*

THOMAS JEFFERSON

A GIFT FOR YOU

One day the poet Thomas Gray
and a friend attended a book
sale, at which a beautifully crafted
bookcase containing a rare
collection of leather-bound French
classics caught Gray's attention.
  'Why don't you buy it?' his
friend asked, to which Gray

replied that he would but that
he couldn't afford the one-
hundred guineas asking price.
Unbeknown to Gray, the Duchess
of Northumberland overheard this
conversation and asked Gray's
friend the identity of the man who
was so interested in the bookcase,
and subsequently bought the
object herself.

Later that day there was a
knock at Gray's door and, much to
his surprise, there on the pavement
stood the bookcase he had so
coveted. Attached to it was a note
apologizing for making so tiny a
gesture in return for the immense
pleasure the Duchess had gained
from reading Gray's 'Elegy Written
in a Country Churchyard'.

'When we honestly ask ourselves
which person in our lives means
the most to us, we often find that it
is those who, instead of giving much
advice, solutions, or cures, have
chosen rather to share our pain
and touch our wounds with a warm
and tender hand. The friend who
can be silent with us in a moment
of despair or confusion, who can
stay with us in an hour of grief
and bereavement, who can tolerate
not knowing, not curing, not
healing and face with us the
reality of our powerlessness,
that is a friend who cares.'

HENRI NOUWEN

UNUSUAL FRIENDS

*You have been my friend. That
in itself is a tremendous thing. I
wove my webs for you because I
liked you. After all, what's a life,
anyway? We're born, we live a little
while, we die. A spider's life can't
help being something of a mess,
with all this trapping and eating
flies. By helping you, perhaps I
was trying to lift up my life a trifle.
Heaven knows anyone's life can
stand a little of that.*

FROM *CHARLOTTE'S WEB*, E. B. WHITE

THESE THREE GIFTS

Surely the most famous gifts of all were those that the three kings brought to the baby Jesus in the manger – gold, frankincense and myrrh. Three Kings' Day is also known as the Epiphany.

'To give without any reward, or any notice, has a special quality of its own.'
ANNE MORROW LINDBERGH

A CHANGE IS AS GOOD AS A REST!

Sometimes one's friends can abandon one, which is precisely what happened to Jacques Soustelle when he was governor-general of Algeria for a year during the 1950s. Writing to the French President, Charles de Gaulle, Soustelle complained that all of his friends were attacking him for supporting de Gaulle's policies in Algeria. Back came the succinct, if rather unhelpful, reply, *'Changez vos amis'* ('change your friends').

UNWANTED GIFTS?

The following is a letter to *The Times* from 23 November, 1988.

Sir,
The worst passed-on present my
father ever received from his eldest
sister was a pair of what looked
like unused bed socks. He, in fury,
gave them to me. When I put them
on I found, to my horror, a used
corn plaster in one of the toe ends.
My aunt, at the time, kept a small
private hotel.

Yours faithfully,
J. B. Prior

REPRINTED IN *A CHRISTMAS CRACKER*,
JOHN JULIUS NORWICH

'I know it's not much, but
it's the best I can do,
My gift is my song and
this one's for you.'
'YOUR SONG' (1970) ELTON JOHN
AND BERNIE TAUPIN

A FAMOUS FRIENDSHIP

Meeting Dr Johnson one day in a
London bookshop, James Boswell
– who at the time was a lawyer –
cultivated the meeting until the two
men had become firm friends.
Some time later they travelled
together to Scotland, prompting
Boswell to write of their journey
in *The Journal of a Tour to*

the Hebrides (1785). Later still, Boswell wrote his famous biography of Johnson, which was published in 1791.

I'M SURE I KNOW HIS WORK …

The eighteenth-century author John Campbell walked into a bookshop one day and became so engrossed in a book that he decided he must buy it. Having taken the book home, he read half of it before realizing … that he had written it.

EQUO NE CREDITE, TEUCRI

Perhaps the most famous gift of all was that given by the Greeks to the Trojans. The following is an excerpt from Virgil's *Aeneid*:

Equo ne credite, Teucri.
Quidquid id est, timeo Danaos et dona ferentes.

Do not trust the horse, Trojans. Whatever it is, I fear the Greeks even when they bring gifts.

A TRULY BYRONIC ACT

When studying at Harrow School Lord Byron was great friends with Robert Peel. One day, seeing Peel about to get beaten by a senior boy at the school, Byron, who had no hope of fighting the older boy off, incapacitated as he was by his club foot, instead demanded to know how many stripes the boy was going to inflict upon his poor friend.

'What's that to you?' asked the senior boy angrily.

'Because,' replied Byron, his voice shaking with anger, 'I would take half.'

'We've got this gift of love, but love
is like a precious plant. You can't
just accept it and leave it in the
cupboard or just think it's going to
get on by itself. You've got to keep
watering it. You've got to really look
after it and nurture it.'

JOHN LENNON

ONE PERFECT ROSE

Why is it no one ever sent me yet
One perfect limousine,
do you suppose?
Ah no, it's always just my luck to get
One perfect rose.

DOROTHY PARKER

TIPS ON WRITING A THANK-YOU LETTER

Write your note promptly after the event – it's no good leaving it for months, do it as soon as possible.

◆

Use attractive postcards for your thank yous – that way the recipient gets a warm and fuzzy feeling from the note itself *and* the lovely picture!

◆

Always hand-write your note – focus on who you are writing to and make it as personal as possible.

◆

Remember it's the thought that counts: always write an upbeat

note, even if you hate the jumper
that Gran knitted, or the floral tie
from Auntie Sylvia.

◆

If you have received money or a
token, let the gift giver know what
you have spent their gift on (or put
it towards).

◆

If you don't want to write
too much, enclose a recent
photograph.

*'Never look a gift horse
in the mouth.'*
PROVERB

WONDERFUL GIFTS

Colombian novelist Gabriel García Márquez is said to have been a great friend of Cuba's Fidel Castro, who was a great admirer of the writer's novels – so much so, in fact, that when Márquez won the Nobel Prize for Literature in 1982, Castro sent 1,500 bottles of Cuban rum to Stockholm where Márquez received the award.

'Happiness is not so much in having as sharing. We make a living by what we get, but we make a life by what we give.'

NORMAN MacEWAN

TOO EXPENSIVE!

While travelling in Paris in 1778,
British ambassador the Earl of
Albemarle took with him his
mistress Lolotte Gaucher who,
several contemporary sources
claim, was both clever and greedy.

One evening, after a
particularly sumptuous meal,
the Earl caught sight of his
beloved gazing up at a bright
star in the sky.

'It's no good,' he is reported to
have said. 'I can't buy it for you.'

LOVE AND FRIENDSHIP

Love is like the wild rose-briar;
Friendship like the holly-tree.
The holly is dark when the
rose-briar blooms,
But which will bloom most
constantly?

The wild rose-briar is
sweet in spring,
Its summer blossoms scent the air;
Yet wait till winter comes again,
And who will call the
wild-briar fair?

Then scorn the silly
rose-wreath now,
And deck thee with

the holly's sheen,
That, when December
blights thy brow,
He may still leave thy
garland green.

EMILY BRONTË

'Make new friends, but
don't forget the old ones.'
YIDDISH PROVERB

FRIENDS IN HIGH PLACES

One of the many jobs US President Abraham Lincoln had to deal with every week was the appeals for pardon that came to him from soldiers who were due to be disciplined by the military. As a matter of precedent, each appeal usually came with a bundle of letters from the man's friends and other people of influence in support of him. However one day an appeal landed on Lincoln's desk with nothing attached.

'What!' the President is said to have shouted, 'Has this man no friends?'

'No sir, not one,' came the reply.

'Then,' said Lincoln, 'I will be his friend.'

FAMOUS FRIENDSHIPS

Dr Johnson and James Boswell

◆

Charlotte Brontë and
Elizabeth Gaskell

◆

Ernest Hemingway and
F. Scott Fitzgerald

◆

Sir Edmund Hillary and
Sherpa Tenzing

◆

Bonnie and Clyde

Abbott and Costello

•

Butch Cassidy and the
Sundance Kid

•

Jean Paul Sartre and
Simone de Beauvoir

•

David Niven and Errol Flynn

•

Laurel and Hardy

*'In giving, a man receives
more than he gives, and the
more is in proportion to the
worth of the thing given.'*
GEORGE MACDONALD

THE GREATEST GIFT?

American travel writer Bill Bryson
once told of his great friendship
with producer Allan Sherwin,
whom he met for a drink one
night, just before setting off for a
trip to Australia.

'I mentioned,' wrote Bryson,
'my plans on the next trip to tackle
the formidable desert regions
alone … In order to deepen his
admiration for me, I had told him
some vivid stories of travellers
who had come unstuck in the
unforgiving interior.

One of these had pertained
to an expedition in the 1850s
led by a surveyor named Robert
Austin, which grew so lost and
short of water in the arid wastes

beyond Mt. Magnet in Western
Australia that the members were
reduced to drinking their own
and their horses' urine. The story
affected him so powerfully that he
announced at once the intention to
accompany me through the most
perilous parts of the present trip,
in the role of driver and scout.'

As reported, Sherwin did
join Bryson on a later trip to
Northern Queensland where, very
generously, he told Bryson, 'I just
want you to know that if it comes
to it you may have all of my urine.'

❦❦❦❦❦❦❦❦❦

❦❦❦

'He that gives all, though but little,
gives much; because God looks not
to the quantity of the gift, but to the
quality of the giver.'

FRANCIS QUARLES

❦❦❦

FAMOUS FICTIONAL
FRIENDSHIPS

Sherlock Holmes and
Doctor Watson

◆

Peter Pan and Wendy

◆

Piglet and Pooh

❦❦❦❦❦❦❦❦❦

Charlie Brown and Snoopy

•

Lone Ranger and Tonto

•

Tom Sawyer and Huckleberry Finn

•

Jack and Jill

•

Sooty and Sweep

•

Tom and Jerry

•

Asterix and Obelisk

'Not that which we give,
but what we share –
For the gift without the
giver is bare.'
JAMES RUSSELL LOWELL

ENOUGH FRIENDS

Normally, people think that there's no such thing as having too many friends, but this was not something that seemed to bother Max Beckman – the early-twentieth-century German Expressionist artist. The professors at the university at which Beckman was lecturing wanted to throw a party in his honour, and so sent an emissary over to the Beckmans' house to proffer their invitation. Answering the door, Mrs Beckman said she had better just check with her husband, only to return a few minutes later to say that the answer was, 'No, thank you. He has enough friends already.'

ARABIAN PROVERB

*A friend is one to whom one may
pour out all the contents of one's
heart, chaff and grain together,
knowing that the gentlest of hands
will take and sift it, keep what is
worth keeping and, with a breath
of kindness, blow the rest away.*

FOUR THINGS MAKE
US HAPPY HERE

*'Health is the first good lent to men;
A gentle disposition then:
Next, to be rich by no by-ways;
Lastly, with friends t' enjoy our days.'*

ROBERT HERRICK

WE LOVE EACH OTHER

Infamously, Hollywood film producer Samuel Goldwyn did not get on too well with that other lion of Hollywood, Louis B. Mayer.

One day, in the locker room of the Hillcrest County Club in Los Angeles, it was said that Mayer, having Goldwyn in a corner of the room, subsequently pushed him into a laundry basket. Later on a friend commented on the incident to Goldwyn, saying how disappointed he was that the two men didn't get along.

Goldwyn was apparently astonished, '*What*?' he gasped. 'We're like friends! We're like

brothers! We love each other!
We'd do anything for each other.
We'd even cut each other's throats
for each other!'

*The worst gift is a fruitcake.
There is only one fruitcake in the
entire world, and people keep
sending it to each other.'*

JOHNNY CARSON, *THE TONIGHT SHOW*

ONE GIFT DESERVES ANOTHER!

British artist P. Tennyson Cole once recorded the following rather extraordinary story concerning gifts: 'I received a commission to paint a beautiful lady who counted millionaires among her admirers.

' "You know, Mr Cole," she said when she handed me the final payment, "this has been an excellent picture, really most valuable. I showed it to Mr A (mentioning the name of a millionaire) and of course he bought it for me. Then I showed it to Mr B (mentioning the name of a second millionaire) and he bought it for me as well. So you see, I give

you five hundred guineas, and I
have got five hundred guineas
as well." '

GRANDMA'S GIFT

Johnny's grandmother, Yvanka,
gave her grandson two beautifully
hand-knitted sweaters for
Hanukkah one year. When Johnny
went to visit Yvanka a few months
later, he made certain he was
wearing one of them. But when
he turned up on the doorstep,
instead of being greeted with
smiles and hugs by his granny,
Yvanka said, 'What? You didn't
like the other one?'

RETURN TO SENDER

Some gifts are simply not wanted, as Zsa Zsa Gabor very eloquently pointed out on a TV show where guest celebrities were supposed to help viewers sort out their marital difficulties. A woman rang in to explain that she had recently broken off her engagement to a wealthy man who had given her a fur coat, diamond jewellery, a stove and a Rolls-Royce.'

'What should I do?' she asked Gabor.

'Send back the stove,' replied Zsa Zsa.

'Books and friends should
be few but good.'
PROVERB

SAY IT WITH FLOWERS

One day, Michael was passing
by a florist's shop when he saw a
large sign in the window saying,
'Say It With Flowers'. Going into
the shop, he asked the assistant to
wrap one pink rose for him to buy.

'Only one?' asked the assistant.

'Just one,' Michael replied.

'I'm a man of few words.'

❧❧❧

'Yesterday is history. Tomorrow is a mystery. And today? Today is a gift. That's why we call it the present.'

BABATUNDE OLATUNJI

❧❧❧

HUNTER-GATHERERS

There's definitely a difference in the techniques employed by men and women when it comes to the buying of gifts, a difference which the following observation by writer Cynthia Heimel is at pains to point out!

'You know men's problem? They're hunters. We're gatherers. We browse, they run in and buy the first thing they see. What they really want to do is walk in with a big bloody buck on their shoulders, plop it at our feet and say, "Merry Christmas".'

❦

'We are always too busy for our children; we never give them the time or interest they deserve. We lavish gifts upon them but the most precious gift, our personal association, which means so much to them, we give grudgingly.'

MARK TWAIN

❦

UNAPPRECIATED GIFTS

According to several sources, when the first edition of Edward Gibbon's *Decline and Fall of the Roman Empire* was published in 1776 the author gifted a copy to the Duke of Gloucester (brother to King George III). On publishing a second volume some ten years later, Gibbon then gave the Duke the second book, only to be met with the rather off-putting reply, 'Another damned, thick, square book! Always scribble, scribble, scribble! Eh, Mr Gibbon?'

PUT SOME FIZZ INTO IT!

When celebrating any occasion champagne is the premier drink of choice, so here's a short (actually rather long!) guide to the sizes of champagne bottles from which to choose:

Split or Piccolo – 187.5 or 200 ml, a quarter-bottle

◆

Demi – 375 ml, a half-bottle

◆

Imperial – 750 ml, a bottle

◆

Magnum – 1.5 lts, two bottles

◆

Jeroboam – 3 lts, four bottles

Rehoboam – 4.5 lts, six bottles

•

Methuselah – 6 lts, eight bottles

•

Salmanazar – 9 lts, 12 bottles

•

Balthazar – 12 lts, 16 bottles

•

Nebuchadnezzar – 15 lts,
20 bottles

•

Melchior – 18 lts, 24 bottles

•

Solomon – 25 lts, 33.3 bottles

•

Primat – 27 lts, 36 bottles

•

Melchizedek – 30 lts, 40 bottles

'An excellent present for almost
anyone is a Book Token, which
you can buy, combined with a
greeting-card at most bookshops
from 3s. 6d. upwards, and which
the recipient exchanges for a book
of her choice at her local shop.'

ELIZABETH CRAIG

'Everyone is gifted – but
some people never open
their package'
ANONYMOUS

'Now, Mrs Dixon,' said the doctor, 'you say you have shooting pains in your neck, dizziness and constant nausea. Just for the record, how old are you?'

'I'm going to be thirty-nine at my next birthday, doctor,' the woman replied indignantly.

'Hmmm,' muttered the doctor, 'got a slight case of memory loss, too …'

BIBLIOGRAPHY

Braude, Jacob, *Braude's Handbook of Stories for Toastmasters and Speakers*, Prentice-Hall, Inc, 1980

Fadiman, Clifton (ed), *The Faber Book of Anecdotes*, Faber & Faber, 1985

Fuller, Nigel, *2,500 Anecdotes for All Occasions*, Avenel Books, 1980

Knowles, Elizabeth (ed), *The Oxford Dictionary of Quotations*, Oxford University Press, 2001

Opie, Iona and Peter, *The Oxford Nursery Rhyme Book*, Oxford University Press, 1973

ALSO AVAILABLE IN
THIS SERIES:

Rees, Nigel, *Cassell Dictionary of Anecdotes*, Cassell, 2000

Metcalf, Fred (ed), *The Penguin Dictionary of Modern Humorous Quotations*, Penguin, 1986

Minkoff, David, *The Ultimate Book of Jewish Jokes*, Robson Books, 2007

WEBSITES

www.anecdotage.com

www.brainyquote.com

www.friendship.com

www.wisdomquotes.com

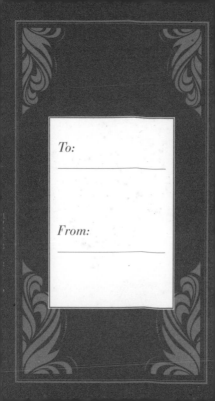

To:
_____

From:
_____